Diet recommendations during TCM - Liver - Wind with Blood Deficiency

Please check these recommendations always with a nutrition consultant, therapist, doctor or dietician. The recipes and the list of ingredients are supporting the conventional medical therapy. The calorie disclosures of fresh ingredients (fruit and vegetables) vary according to quality and time of harvest. The contents were checked by a dietician and a nutrition consultant for the Traditional Chinese Medicine (TCM).

Author:
©2020 Josef Miligui
www.ebns.at

AF220847

Source:
The lists are created from the EBNS database for nutritional counseling. The database is used by dietitians, therapists and doctors for advising the patient / client.

Literature:
The specialist literature and the training documents of the German and Austrian dietary and traditional Chinese medicine serve as a knowledge base. We have used the documents as a basis of knowledge, adapted it to our experience and completed them.
http://nutribook.info/

Production and publishing:
BoD – Books on Demand, Norderstedt
ISBN: 9783752857245

Diet recommendations for TCM - Liver - Wind with Blood Deficiency

1   Treatment strategy

Foods that disperse wind.

2   Avoid

n.a.

3   Breakfast

	kkal. per serving
Celery juice	33
Celery soup	101
Fennel-Rice Soup	155
Spelled-grid porridge with berries of the season	24
Tea from lavender blossoms	0
Tea from savory	1

4   Snack

Spelled-grid porridge with berries of the season	243

5   Lunch

Celery and potato cream soup	112
Celery juice	33
Celery salad with lemon and olive oil	402
Celery soup	101
Chicory salad with tangerine	256
Fennel and potato gratin	147
Fennel with roasted walnuts	342
Fennel-Rice Soup	155
Spelled-grid porridge with berries of the season	243
Tea from lavender blossoms	0
Tea from savory	1

6 Afternoon

7 Dinner

8 Any time

9 Recipes

(rec.) = You can use more.
(little) = You should use less than specified
(omit) = omit.

9.1 Basic recipe for a reissue soup (Congee)

Warms the stomach and spleen, harmonizes the intestine, forces Qi, reduces moisture.
Cooking time approx. 2-4 hours
Calories p. portion: 140
3 portions

Quantity of ingredients
Rice variety any 1 cup / 120g. (yes) - warm - sweet .... metal
Water 6 cups / 700g. (yes) - cool - salty .... earth

Cooking instructions:
Cook rice and water in a ratio of about 1: 6. The amount of water determines the thickness of the mash (matter of taste).
Put the rice in a saucepan with a heavy lid. It is important to simmer the rice after a short boil on the slightest flame, otherwise it burns.
Boil the rice for 2-4 hours. The longer he cooks, the more he strengthens.
If you want to eat the dish for breakfast, you can put the rice on just before bedtime.
To be on the safe side, you should first check the behavior of your pot and cooker under observation for a similar amount of time, so that nothing burns.
Refrigerate for later use.

9.2 Basic recipe for a vegetable soup, nutritious

Strengthens spleen and lung, regulates Qi flow, builds up Qi, dries out, passes downwardly, strengthens stomach Qi.
Cooking time approx. 2-3 hours
Calories p. portion: 48
5 portions
Allergens: L

Quantity of ingredients

Olive oil 1 table spoon / 4g. (little) - cool - sweet .... earth
Onion white 1 piece / 60g. (little) - warm - acrid .... metal
Carrot 3 pieces / 200g. (yes) - neutral - sweet .... earth
Parsnip 3/8 lbs - 6oz / 150g. (yes) - cool - bitter... fire
Celery root 1 cup / 100g. (rec.) - cool - sweet .... earth
Ginger fresh 1/2 teaspoon / 2g. (little) - warm - acrid .... metal
Lemon 1/2 piece / 25g. (rec.) - cold - sour .... wood
Juniper berry 6 pieces / 6g. () - warm - sweet, acrid, bitter .... fire
Thyme dried 1 pinch / 1g. (little) - warm - bitter... metal
Lovage 1 table spoon / 3g. () - warm - acrid, bitter.................................... metal
Bay leaf 2 leaves / 1g. (yes) - warm - acrid .... *
Salt 1 pinch / 1g. (little) - cold - salty .... water
Water 3 cups / 650g. (yes) - cool - salty... earth

Cooking instructions:

Cut the vegetables into cubes.
Heat oil in hot pot, fry shortly onions and vegetables.
Add cold water, then add ginger, bay leaf and lemon juice.
Season with juniper, thyme and lovage. Cover for 2 - 3 hours on a low
heat and simmer.
The used vegetables should be thrown away.
The basic recipe serves as a soup base and to refine vegetables,
legumes or cereals.
If you want to eat vegetable soup immediately, add the desired
vegetables half an hour before.
Refrigerate for later use.

9.3   Celery and potato cream soup

Strengthens spleen and liver, regulates Qi flow, strengthens stomach
Qi, forces Qi, relieves inflammation, relaxes, dissolves stagnation.
Cooking time approx. 45 min
Calories p. portion: 113
4 portions
Allergens: GL

Quantity of ingredients

Olive oil 1 table spoon / 10g. (little) - cool - sweet .... earth
Onion white 1/2 piece / 25g. (little) - warm - acrid .... metal
Basic recipe for a vegetable soup 3 cups / 700g. (yes) - neutral - * ....*
Potato 5/8 oz / 200g. (yes) - neutral - sweet .... earth
Nutmeg 1 pinch / 0,5g. (little) - warm - acrid .... metal
Ground 1 pinch / 0,5g. (little) - warm - acrid .... metal
Lemon peel 1/4 piece / 1g. (little) - cool - bitter .... fire

Créme fraiche cheese 2 table spoons / 20g. (little) - neutral - sweet .... earth
Salt 1 pinch / 1g. (little) - cold - salty .... water
Parsley 1 table spoon / 8g. (rec.) - warm - bitter ....wood

Cooking instructions:
Heat the olive oil in a saucepan lightly. Fry the onions very gently in a mild heat. Pour with vegetable stock according to the basic recipe. Cover and cook for 15 minutes.
Add curd-cut potato, celery, nutmeg, cumin and lemon zest. Spice with salt and cook for 12 minutes. Potatoes and celery should be soft.
Remove the lemon peel.
Puree the soup with crème fraiche using a blender. Season the soup with salt.
Arrange the soup in portions with the chopped parsley.

9.4   Celery juice

Strengthens stomach Qi, moisturizes, relaxes, builds up Qi, spreads.
Cooking time approx. 5 min
Calories p. portion: 33
1 portions
Allergens: L

Quantity of ingredients
Celery root 1/2 piece / 200g. (rec.) - cool - sweet .... earth
Water 1 cup / 120g. (yes) - cool - salty.. earth
Salt 1 pinch / 0,5g. (little) - cold - salty .... water

Cooking instructions:
Peel celeriac and cut into pieces and juice. Mix with water and salt as needed.

9.5   Celery salad with lemon and olive oil

Strengthens stomach Qi, moisturizes, relaxes, builds up Qi.
Cooking time approx. 10 min
Calories p. portion: 402
1 portions
Allergens: L

Quantity of ingredients

Celery root 1/2 piece / 200g. (rec.) - cool - sweet .... earth
Lemon juice 1/2 piece / 10g. (rec.) - cold - sour .... wood
Olive oil 4 table spoons / 40g. (little) - cool - sweet .... earth

Cooking instructions:

Peel celeriac and cut into pieces and rub. Serve with the lemon juice and olive oil.

9.6   Celery soup

Refreshing, builds up fluids and Qi.
Cooking time approx. 45 min
Calories p. portion: 101
4 portions
Allergens: ACGL

Quantity of ingredients

Water 2 cup / 500g. (yes) - cool - salty .... earth
Butter organic 1 table spoon / 15g. (yes) - neutral - sweet .... earth
Nutmeg 1 pinch / 1g. (little) - warm - acrid .... metal
Salt 1 pinch / 1g. (little) - cold - salty .... water
Spelled wholemeal flour 2-3 teaspoons / 25g. (little) - neutral - sweet .... wood
Celery root 1 piece / 500g. (rec.) - cool - sweet .... earth
Chicken egg 1 piece / 55g. (little) - neutral - sweet .... earth
Cream sour 10% 2 table spoons / 25g. (little) - neutral - sweet .... earth
Celery sticks 2 table spoons / 20g. (yes) - cool - sweet .... earth
Pepper (ground) 1 pinch / 0,5g. () - warm - acrid .... metal

Cooking instructions:

In a hot saucepan, melt 1 tbsp butter; add a pinch of nutmeg, a pinch of salt, 1/2 cup wholegrain spelled flour (finely ground as fresh as possible) and stir to a sweat while stirring; add 1/2 liter of hot water gradually; add 1 large finely chopped celery tuber; cook for about 35 minutes and then puree; mix 1 egg yolk with 1 cup of cream; in the hot - no longer boiling! - soup vigorously; add some celery leaves finely chopped; with pepper, salt to taste.

9.7   Chicory salad with tangerine

Nourishing builds up fluids, in the absence of blood and lack of heart and liver fluids, emits moist heat down. Not
 with middle-Qi deficiency.
Cooking time approx. 10 min
Calories p. portion: 257
3 portions
Allergens: AGNO

Quantity of ingredients
Tangerine 4 pieces / 300g. (little) - cool - sweet, sour .... wood
Chicory 2-3 pieces / 300g. (rec.) - cool - sweet, bitter .... fire
Sesame oil 2 table spoons / 18g. (yes) - cool - sweet .... earth
Pepper (ground) 1 pinch / 0,5g. () - warm - acrid .... metal
Salt 1 pinch / 1g. (little) - cold - salty .... water
Vinegar Aceto Balsamico 2 teaspoons / 6g. (yes) - warm - sour, bitter ..... wood
Orange 1/2 piece / 70g. (little) - cold - sour, sweet .... wood
Lemon 1/2 piece / 25g. (rec.) - cold - sour .... wood
Orange jam 1 teaspoon / 4g. () - cool - sour, sweet .... wood
Cream, sweet 30% 1 table spoon / 10g. (little) - neutral - sweet .... earth
White bread (wheat bread) 6 slices / 120g. (yes) - cool - sweet .... wood

Cooking instructions:
Peel tangerines and cut into bite-sized pieces; Cut chicory roughly and mix well.
Dressing: sesame oil, pepper, salt, raspberry vinegar or balsamic vinegar, a little lemon or orange juice, rose paprika, orange marmalade or, alternatively, another jam, stir well. Give a little sweet cream over the salad and let it pass briefly.

9.8   Fennel and potato gratin

Regulates Qi, warms the inside, lowers cold, forces stomach, relieves constipation, forces Yang, dissolves mucus, reduces wind, spreads. forces Qi, forces spleen, relaxes, builds up Qi, spreads.
Cooking time approx. 1 1/2 hours
Calories p. portion: 147
2 portions
Allergens: CGL

Quantity of ingredients

Fennel 5/8 oz / 200g. (yes) - warm - sweet, little acrid .... earth
Potato 1/4 lbs - 4oz / 125g. (yes) - neutral - sweet .... earth
Basic recipe for a vegetable soup (nutritious) 1/2 cup / 100g. (yes) - neutral - **
Butter organic 1 teaspoon / 3g. (yes) - neutral - sweet .... earth
Rice flour 2 teaspoons / 6g. (yes) - warm - sweet .... metal
Cream sour 10% 1 teaspoon / 3g. (little) - neutral - sweet .... earth
Salt 1 pinch / 1g. (little) - cold - salty .... water
Sugar cane sugar 1 pinch / 1g. () - cool - sweet .... earth
Chicken yolk 1 piece / 10g. (rec.) - neutral - sweet .... earth
Pepper Cayenne 1 pinch / 0,5g. () - warm - acrid .... metal
Nutmeg 1 pinch / 0,5g. (little) - warm - acrid .... metal
Parsley 1 teaspoon / 2g. (rec.) - warm - bitter .... wood
Chives 1 teaspoon / 3g. (little) - warm - acrid .... metal
Butter organic 1 teaspoon / 3g. (yes) - neutral - sweet .... earth

Cooking instructions:

Cook peeled potatoes and then let cool. Wash the fennel, cut off the stems and remove any outer leaves.
Hold back fennel greens and add it to the sauce with the other herbs later.
Steam the fennel tubers for about 15 - 20 minutes.
Then cut the potatoes and fennel into slices and place in layers in a greased baking dish.
Bring the liquid of fennel broth to the boil and bind it with flour.
Season with sea salt, cayenne pepper, sugar, nutmeg and sour cream.
Allow to cool and alloy with egg yolk.
Spread the sauce over the casserole, sprinkle with parmesan and finely chopped parsley and chives. Bake at 200 °C / 392 °F in the oven for half an hour.

9.9   Fennel with roasted walnuts

Regulates Qi, warms the inside, lowers coldness, strengthens the stomach, relieves constipation, strengthens kidneys and spleen Yang, dissolves mucus, reduces wind, reduce cold evil, soften knots, strengthens stomach Qi.
Cooking time approx. 20 min
Calories p. portion: 342
4 portions
Allergens: HO

Quantity of ingredients
Fennel 4 pieces / 800g. (yes) - warm - sweet, little acrid .... earth
Nutmeg 1 pinch / 1g. (little) - warm - acrid .... metal
Ginger fresh 1/2 teaspoon / 1g. (little) - warm - acrid .... metal
Salt 1 pinch / 1g. (little) - cold - salty .... water
White wine 1/2 cup / 125g. (yes) - cool - sweet, bitter, acrid .... wood
Olive oil 2 table spoons / 40g. (little) - cool - sweet .... earth
Walnuts 2 table spoons / 35g. (rec.) - warm - sweet .... earth
Water 1 1/2 cups / 220g. (yes) - cool - salty .... earth
Corn Grease (Polenta) 1 cup / 120g. (yes) - neutral - sweet .... earth
Salt 1 pinch / 1g. (little) - cold - salty .... water

Cooking instructions:
Heat very little water in a pot; Fry the fennel in strips. Add Nutmeg, a little grated ginger, add salt, a dash of white wine, rose paprika.
Simmer until the vegetables are cooked, but still crisp; stir in a little olive oil; sprinkle with roasted walnuts.

Stir the polenta into a pot of hot water, stirring constantly, until the polenta has the desired consistency. Salt.
Pull the polenta off the fire and let it swell for about 10 minutes.

9.10 Fennel-Rice Soup

Regulates Qi, warms the inside, lowers cold, forces stomach, relieves constipation, forces Yang, dissolves mucus, reduces wind, spreads, strengthens Qi and kidney Jing, builds up Qi.
Cooking time approx. 15-20 min
Calories p. portion: 156
2 portions
Allergens: EG

Quantity of ingredients
Basic recipe for a rice soup (Congee) 1 cup / 300g. (yes) - neutral - sweet ..... *
Fennel 1/2 piece / 150g. (yes) - warm - sweet, little acrid .... earth
Butter organic 1 table spoon / 15g. (yes) - neutral - sweet .... earth
Soy sauce 1 dash / 3g. (little) - cold - salty .... water

Cooking instructions:
Cook the fennel softly in the rice soup according to the basic recipe.
Before serving, add a piece of butter and some soy sauce.

9.11 Spelled-grid porridge with berries of the season

Nourishes fluids, moisturises dryness, produces humors, moisturizes intestines, cools inner heat, preserves the fluids, contracts, forces middle, nourishes heart and liver-blood, preserves the fluids, contracts.
Cooking time approx. 15 min
Calories p. portion: 244
2 portions
Allergens: AGH

Quantity of ingredients
Cow's milk (1.5% fat) 1/2 cup / 125g. (yes) - neutral - sweet .... earth
Water 1/2 cup / 125g. (yes) - cool - salty.. earth
Spelled semolina 5 table spoons / 50g. (little) - neutral - sweet .... wood
Butter organic 2 teaspoons / 20g. (yes) - neutral - sweet........................... earth
Berries of the season 1/4 lbs - 4oz / 100g. (yes) - neutral - sweet, sour .... wood
Honey 1-2 teaspoons / 5g. () - cold - sweet .... earth
Almond 1-2 teaspoons / 5g. (yes) - neutral - sweet.................................... earth
Peppermint 3-4 leaves / 2g. (yes) - cool - acrid, bitter............................... metal
Cinnamon ground 1 pinch / 0,5g. () - hot - acrid, sweet ....*
Vanilla 1 pinch / 0,2g. (yes) - neutral - sweet ....*
Cocoa 1 pinch / 0,5g. () - warm - sweet, bitter .... fire
Coconut grated 1 table spoon / 10g. (rec.) - warm - sweet .... earth

Cooking instructions:
Stir in spelled semolina in cold water and boil slowly over medium heat. After boiling, remove from the heat and let simmer for a few minutes. Depending on the desired consistency, some water may have to be added. Stir in the butter and fine grated nuts in the mash and raspberries. Serve with honey or whole-grain sugar as desired.
Spices and aromas: fresh mint, cinnamon or vanilla, cocoa, coconut

Summer: raspberries, blueberries, strawberries

9.12 Tea from chamomile

Reduces internal wind and heat, cools liver.
Cooking time approx. 10 min
Calories p. portion: 0
1 portions

Quantity of ingredients
Chamomile 1 teaspoon / 3g. (yes) - cool - sweet, bitter ....*
Water 1 cup / 120g. (yes) - cool - salty... earth

Cooking instructions:
Heat the water till it boils and put it aside. Chamomile flowers added and 10 min. to let go.

9.13 Tea from lavender blossoms

Cooking time approx. 10 min
Calories p. portion: 0
1 portions

Quantity of ingredients
Lavender blossoms 1 teaspoon / 2g. (yes) - warm - acrid, bitter ....*
Water 1 cup / 125g. (yes) - cool - salty.. earth

Cooking instructions:
Heat the water till it boils and put it aside. Add lavender flowers and 10 min. to let go. Sweet to taste with honey. Strain when pouring.

9.14 Tea from savory

Tonifies the kidney-Yang, the stomach and spleen Qi and warms the middle, forces the liver Qi and the blood, conducts mucus and cold from the lungs, opens the surface, derives wind-cold.
Cooking time approx. 10 min
Calories p. portion: 1
4 portions

Quantity of ingredients
Savory 2-4 teaspoons / 9g. (rec.) - warm - bitter .... water
Water 2 cup / 500g. (yes) - cool - salty.. earth

Cooking instructions:
Brew dried savory with boiling water and cover for about 10 minutes. Strain the tea and drink warm.

10 Effects of food

10.1 Use ingredients: recommendable

Apricot dried
Apricot nectar
Aubergine
Barley
Barley flour
Barley not peeled
Basil
Basil (fresh)
Beef liver
Blackberry´s
Blueberry
Blueberry juice
Calamari
Celery root
Chard
Cherry
Chicken liver
Chicken meat
Chicken yolk
Chicory
Chlorella (fresh water)
Coconut flakes
Coconut grated
Coconut meat
Coriander
Coriander (fresh)
Duck (slaughtered)
Eel
Grape juice red
Grapes red
Grass carp
Hazelnuts
Jasmine blossoms tee
Lamb liver
Leaf salads (bitter)
Lemon
Lemon juice
Millet
Millet flakes
Octopus
Parsley
Parsley root
Passion blossoms tea
Pearl barley
Perch
Plums
Quinoa
Rabbit liver
Radicchio
Raspberry
Red beet
Red berry (without sugar)
Red wine
Rice long grain rice
Rice sweet
Rose blossom tea
Sake
Savory
Sesame paste (Tahini)
Sesame, black
Sesame, white
Shrimp
Spinach
Sunflower seeds
Tsampa (roasted barley flour)
Tuna
Turkey breast meat
Valerian
Walnuts
Water hot
Wheatgrass powder

10.2 Use ingredients: yes

Adzuki beans
Almond
Almond marzipan
Almond milk
Almond puree
Apple (sweet)
Apple juice (natural cloudy)
Apple puree
Apricot
Apricot jam
Apricots
Apricots juice
Arrowroot
Artichoke

Banana
Banana (cooking banana)
Banchatee (green tea)
Barley grass powder
Barley grouts
Basic recipe for a fish soup
Basic recipe for a rice soup (Congee)
Basic recipe for a vegetable soup
(nutritious)
Bay leaf
Beans (green, fresh)
Bearberry leaf
Beef fillet
Beef lungs (calf)
Beef meat
Beef meat (calf)
Beef meatbones
Beef soup meat
Berries of the season
Berry juice
Bitter orange peel
Black beans
Blackberry jam
Blueberry dried
Blueberry jam
Bocksdorn fruits (Fructus Lycii, Goji,
goji berry dried
Boletus mushroom
Borage oil
Breadcrumbs (wheat bread, bread roll)
Broad beans (thick beans)
Broccoli
Buckwheat
Buckwheat (roasted) Kasha
Buckwheat whole grain
Bush beans
Butter (half fat)
Butter beans white
Butter organic
Capers in olive oil
Carob flour, St. john's bread
Carp
Carrot
Carrot (Early Carrot)
Carrot juice without sugar
Cashews
Cauliflower
Celery sticks
Cereal coffee
Chamomile
Champignon
Chanterelle
Cherry (sour)
Cherry compote

Chestnuts
Chicken stomach
Chickpeas
Chinese cabbage
Chrysanthemum blossom tea
Coconut milk
Codfish
Coix (seeds) YiYi Ren
Corn
Corn (fast polenta)
Corn (roasted)
Corn flour
Corn germ oil
Corn Grease (Polenta)
Corn silk tea
Corn starch
Cow's milk (1.5% fat)
Cow's milk (whole milk 3.5% fat)
Cranberry
Cream 10% coffee cream
Cress
Currant jam (black)
Currant jam (red)
Currant juice (black)
Daisy
Dates dried
Dates red
Duck (heart)
Ducks egg
Dulse (seaweed)
Eel smoked
Elderberries
Elderberry blossom tee
Evening primrose oil
Fennel
Fennel seeds ground
Fig
Fig dried
Fish pieces mixed (fresh water)
Flower pollen
Fox nut, gorgon nut, makhana
French beans
Fresh cheese from soya
Gail plum
Gelee Royal
Ginkgo fruit
Ginseng liqueur
Ginseng root
Goose
Goose blood
Goose egg
Goose parts
Gourd
Grape juice white

Grapes white
Grapeseed oil
Herbs various
Herbs wild
Hokkaido pumpkin
Hop
Jellyfish
Kaki plum
Kidney beans (red)
King Solomon's-seal
Kudzu
Lavender blossoms
Lemon Balm (dried)
Lemon Balm (fresh)
Lentils black
Lentils red
Lily bulbs
Lima beans
Lime blossom tea
Linseed
Linseed (crushed)
Linseed oil
Liver smoothing tea
Longane
Luo Han Guo fruit
Lychee
Malt
Manioc flour
Maple syrup
Mare's milk
Miso
Morel (black, dried)
Morel, dried
Mozzarella
Mung bean
Mustard
Mustard Dijon
Mustard medium hot
Mustard sweet
Nasturtium (nose-twister or nose-tweaker)
Noodles (whole grain) with egg
Okra
Olives
Olives green
Oyster mushroom
Oyster shell powder
Oysters
Parmesan
Parsnip
Passion fruit
Peanut (roasted)
Peanut butter
Peanuts

Pear
Pearl barley
Peas
Peas, green
Peppermint
Peppermint tea
Peppers
Pickle
Pigeon
Pine nuts
Pistachios
Pork heart
Pork knuckle
Pork liver
Pork meat
Pork skin
Potato
Potato (mealy)
Potato flour
Psyllium seed
Pumpkin
Pumpkin seeds
Quail
Quail egg
Quince
Rabbit
Rabbit (wild)
Radish
Radish black
Radish horseradish
Raisins
Raspberry leaf tea
Red cabbage
Reishi mushroom
Rice (fragrance)
Rice (Gaoliang / Sorghum)
Rice (whole grain)
Rice Basmati
Rice black
Rice flour
Rice malt
Rice mash
Rice noodles
Rice red
Rice round grain
Rice starch
Rice sticky
Rice variety any
Rice wild (nature rice)
Rye
Rye flour
Rye wholemeal bread
Saffron
Sage

Sago (cereals)
Salsify
Salt (herbal)
Savoy cabbage / kale
Sesame oil
Sesame oil roasted
Shiitake, dried
Soy flour
Soy noodles
Soy Tofu
Soybean milk
Soybeans
Soybeans, black
Soybeans, blacks, fermented
Soybeans, yellow
St. Benedict's thistle, blessed thistle, holy thistle, spotted thistle
Sugar molasses
Sugar substitute (sweetener)
Sweet potato
Trout
Turkey ham
Turnips
Vanilla
Vanilla pod
Vanilla powder
Vanilla sugar natural
Vegetable juice
Vinegar Aceto Balsamico
Vinegar Aceto Balsamico white
Walnuts roasted
Water
Wheat
Wheat bran
Wheat bulgur
Wheat flakes
Wheat flatbread/pita bread
Wheat flour
Wheat flour whole grain
Wheat semolina
Wheat semolina for children
Wheat/Rye/Gray-black bread with yeast
White beans
White bread (pretzel sticks)
White bread (roll)
White bread (wheat bread)
White breadcrumbs
White cabbage
White dumpling bread (wheat bread cut into chunks)
White wine
Whole grain bread
Wholemeal flour
Wild garlic (garlic spinach)
Wormwood herb
Yam root, yam root tuber
Zucchini

10.3 Use ingredients: little

Agar agar (kelp)
Agrimony
Aloe juice
Anise (Common Fennel)
Apple (sour)
Baking powder
Balm
Barley malt
Basic recipe for a beef soup
Basic recipe for a beef soup (warming)
Basic recipe for a chicken soup (warming)
Basic recipe for a duck soup
Batavia
Bean oil
Beef bone marrow
Beef heart
Beef heart (calf)
Beer (alcohol-free)
Beer (alcohol-reduced)
Beer (Pils)
Beer (Top-fermented German dark beer)
Bitter Herb liqueur
Black caraway
Blackberry dried (unripe fruit)
Blackberry leaves
Black-eyed peas
Borage
Bulgur (cereals)
Buttermilk
Cardamom
Caviar
Cherry juice
Chervil
Chervil dried
Chicken egg
Chicken egg white
Chicken heart
Chives
Chocolate
Chocolate (Diabetic)
Clarified butter
Clementine

Clementines
Clove
Coconut fat
Cooking oil
Couscous
Cranberries
Cranberry
Cranberry jam
Cranberry juice
Cream (30% fat)
Cream sour 10%
Cream sour 20%
Cream, sweet 30%
Creamer
Créme fraiche cheese
Cucumber (spicy cucumber)
Cumin (Caraway seed)
Curd cheese 20%
Curd cheese 40%
Currant (black)
Currant (red)
Currant (white)
Currants (black)
Currants (red)
Deer meat
Deer meat
Dill
Emmental cheese
Endive salad
Fennel tea
Fenugreek (Trigonella foenum-graecum)
Feta cheese
Fish innards
Fish sauce
Flounder
Fresh cheese
Fresh cheese with herbs
Freshwater fish
Gelatin white
Ginger fresh
Ginger oil
Goose fat
Gooseberry
Gouda cheese
Green spelt
Ground
Ground caraway
Halibut (Flatfish)
Hawthorn
Hibiscus tea
Iceberg lettuce
Kalmus
Kefir

Kohlrabi
Kombu seaweed (Saccharina japonica)
Kumquats
Lamb's lettuce
Lamb's lettuce
Leek
Lemon peel
Lentils
Lentils yellow
Lettuce
Lobster
Loquate / Japanese medlar
Lotus roots
Lotus seeds
Lovage seeds
Lychee in Preserved
Mallow (Malva sylvestris) blossom tea
Mango juice
Margarine
Margarine (diet)
Marjoram
Mayonnaise 50%
Mediterranean fish (cod, plaice, haddock, sea eel, mackerel)
Medlar
Mirabelle plum
Miso black (fermented)
Miso paste (soy bean paste)
Mulled Wine Spice
Multi-grain bread (gray bread)
Mustard seeds
Nettles
Noodles (wheat) with egg
Noodles (wheat, lasagne) with egg
Noodles (wheat, ribbon noodles) with egg
Noodles (wheat, spaghetti) with egg
Nori, purple seaweed, red algae
Nutmeg
Oat
Oat flakes (whole grain)
Oat flakes roasted
Oat flour
Oat fusion (baby food)
Oat meal
Oat milk
Olive oil
Onion (shallot)
Onion (spring onion)
Onion read
Onion white
Orange
Oregano dried
Oregano fresh

Peaches
Peaches (canned)
Peanut oil
Pear juice
Pepper powder (hot)
Pepperoni
Pepperoni, yellow, pitted, halved
Peppers (sweet)
Peppers powder
Pheasant
Pomegranate
Pork brain
Pork ham
Pork ham cooked
Pork kidneys
Pork lung
Prickly pear
Processed cheese 12%
Puff pastry
Pumpkin seed oil
Rabbit meat
Rapeseed oil
Raspberry dried (immature)
Raspberry jam
Romaine lettuce / lettuce salad
Rose hip
Rose hip tea
Rosemary
Rusk
Salt
Sauerkraut (cutted cabbage fermented)
Shrimps
Sour cherries
Sour cream 15% fat
Sour milk
Sour milk cheese 20%

Soy sauce
Soy Tofu smoked
Soybean oil
Spelled (Dark) bread
Spelled flakes
Spelled grain
Spelled semolina
Spelled wholemeal flour
Spiny lobsters
Star anise
Strawberries
Strawberry jam
Strawberry Juice
Sugar - icing sugar
Sugar brown
Sugar palm sugar
Sunflower oil
Tangerine
Tarragon (Estragon)
Thistle oil
Thyme
Thyme dried
Toast bread (whole grain)
Trout (smoked)
Turmeric (yellow root)
Turnip
Umeboshi plums (Japanese apricots)
Vinegar (Apple vinegar)
Vinegar (Red wine vinegar)
Wakame
Walnut oil
Wax gourd
Wheat germ oil
Wild boar meat
Yeast

10.4 Do not use contra-acting foods

Amaranth
Anchovy / Sardine
Asparagus (green or white)
Avocado
Bamboo shoots
Bitter melon
Black tea
Boxhorn clover seeds
Brussels sprouts
Burdock root tea
Cantaloupe
Carambola (Star fruit)
Chili (pod or ground)
Cinnamon ground
Cinnamon sticks

Cocoa
Cod
Coffee
Crab
Cream sour 30%
Crucian
Cucumber
Curcuma
Curry
Curry paste red
Dandelion (young plants)
Dandelion juice
Dandelionroots tea
Feta cheese
Garlic

Gentian root
Ginger powder
Goat
Goat and sheep's milk
Goat cheese
Gorgonzola
Grapefruit (Pomelo)
Grapefruit juice
Green tea
Herring
Honey
Honey wine (Met)
Hyssop
Juniper berry
Kiwi
Lamb bones
Lamb kidneys
Lamb meat
Lamb shoulder
Lemongrass
Lime
Lovage
Lychee liqueur
Mackerel
Mango
Mineral water
Mold cheese
Mulberry fruit
Mullet
Mung bean sprouting
Mussels
Mutton
Mutton
Octopus
Orange jam
Orange juice
Palm oil
Papaya
Pepper Cayenne
Pepper white (ground)
Peppercorns
Pepperoni, red, pitted, halved

Peppers (rose peppers)
Pimento
Pineapple
Pineapple (from a can)
Pineapple juice without sugar
Plaice
Plum
Plum dried
Poppy
Pork Bacon
Pork ham smoked
Pork Lard
processed cheese 30%
Radish (white, green, purple-red)
Rhubarb
Rosefish
Salmon
Seacrab
Shark
Sheep's milk
Sheep's milk yoghurt
Sorrel
Spirit
Sugar candy white
Sugar cane sugar
Sugar fructose - fruit sugar
Sugar glucose - grapes sugar
Sugar Milk Sugar
Sugar white
Tomato
Tomato dried
Tomato juice
Tomato paste
Tomato puree
Watermelon
Wheat beer
Yarrow
Yarrow tea
Yoghurt vanilla
Yogi tea
Yogurt (natural, 1.5% fat)
Yogurt (natural, 3.5% fat)

11 Complementary

11.1 Cinnamon bark

Cinnamomum verum, cort.
Preparation: Decoction
Warms channels, promotes yang and channel flow, reduces cold evil, tonifies yang energy and warms.
Decoction from 2-5 g, drink in two doses on an empty stomach; to increase the effect, add 2 g licorice root and 3 slices of ginseng.
Special features: In TCM, cinnamon is a very good supplement for many other herbs, especially for yang tonic. It enhances the warming and toning properties of herbal tinctures and improves their taste. Cinnamon is one of the most warming remedies in Chinese herbal medicine, it warms cold extremities and also internal organs
Do not use together with: onions and kaolin.

11.2 Ginger fresh

Zingiberis officinalis, Rhizoma
Preparation: Decoction
Strengthens juices production, reduces cold-nuisance, stimulates, stimulates the Yang-energy, warms the lung- and stomach-energy.
Put 1-6 slices of fresh root in a jug of water for 3 minutes. Drink 10 g in two doses on empty stomach.
To improve the taste is brown raw sugar
Special features: In TCM, the fresh ginger root is mainly used against fish poisoning and colds of the lungs and stomach. Because ginger promotes nutrient uptake, it is often used in a variety of formulations to facilitate the rapid absorption of other herbs and thereby enhance their effects. Ginger contains the digestive enzyme zingibain. The digestive effect of this substance is stronger than that of the enzyme papain.
In too large quantities, ginger leads to constipation, Not to use in: pregnancy, high fever.

12 Basics of Nutrition
The basic principles of nutrition described herein are general recommendations. They are not aimed at a specific form of therapy.

Recommendations concerning a therapy have priority.

12.1 Nutrition

Regular meals in a relaxed atmosphere. A warm breakfast is considered a good start into the day.
The main meals ought to be taken for lunch – supper in the early evening. Pay attention to feeling hungry or sated: don't eat too much nor remain hungry is the rule
Prepare the meals freshly from natural, regional products. Frozen, heat-conserved, industrially prepared or foodstuffs cooked in the microwave oven are rejected.
Choice of foodstuffs according to the season: more cooling food in summer, more warming food in winter.
Eat cooked food at least twice a day. Food and drinks ought to be lukewarm, never ice-cold or hot.
Raw vegetables, briefly cooked vegetables, freshly squeezed juices and mineral water are not recommended. Milk and dairy products are only included in the diet if they don't cause problems. Don't use therapeutic recipes over a longer period without consulting your doctor or therapist.

Varied food
Enjoy the diversity of foodstuffs. Characteristics of a balanced nutrition are variety, suitable combination and a balanced quantity of rich and low energy foodstuffs (on one hand avoiding undersupply with essential nutrients and on the other hand to take to many undesirable substances).

A lot of Cereal Products - and Potatoes
Bread, pasta, rice, cereal flakes (best wholemeal) as well as potatoes contain almost no fat, but many vitamins, mineral nutrients, trace elements, roughage and secondary plant substances. These foodstuffs ought to be taken with low-fat side dishes.

Vegetables and Fruit – „Take Five" every day ... 5 portions of vegetables and fruit a day, as fresh as possible, briefly cooked, or maybe one portion as a juice – ideal as a side dish to every meal as well as snack between meals: Thus a lot of vitamins, mineral nutrients as well as roughage and secondary plant substances

Daily milk and dairy products
Milk and Dairy Products every Day, once or twice per Week Fish; meat, sausages as well as eggs moderately. These foodstuffs contain valuable nutrients like calcium in the milk, iodine selenium and omega-3

fat acids in saltwater fish. Meat is favorable due to its high content of disposable iron and the vitamins B1, B6 and B12. Quantities of 300 – 600 g meat and sausage per week are sufficient. Prefer low-fat products, especially in meat- and dairy products.

Low-fat and fatty Foodstuffs
Fat supplies us with essential fat acids and fatty foodstuffs contain also fat-soluble vitamins. Fat is high in energy; therefore much fat in the food may cause overweight, possibly also cancer. Too many saturated fat acids may further a tendency for cardio-vascular diseases in the long term. Prefer vegetable oils and fats (e.g. rapeseed-, olive-, soya-oils and solid fats produced therefrom). Beware of invisible fat in meat- and dairy products, pastry and sweets as well as in fast-food and convenience foods. 70 – 90 g fat per day is sufficient.

Moderately Sugar and Salt
Take sugar and foods/drinks containing various kinds of sugar (e.g. glucose syrup) only occasionally. Use herbs and spices as well as a little salt creatively. Prefer salt containing iodine.

Plenty of Liquids
Water is absolutely essential. Drink 1-2 l liquids every day. Prefer water (with or without gas) and other low-calorie drinks. Alcoholic drinks should not be taken.

Tasty Dishes, carefully cooked
Cook the meals with as low temperatures and as short as possible, using little water and fat – this preserves the original taste, keeps the nutrients intact and prevents the production of harmful compounds.

Take time and enjoy the food
Take your Time and enjoy your Food
Eating consciously helps to eat right. The eye enjoys food, too. It's fun, invites to enjoy varied dishes and stimulates the feeling of satiety.

Watch your Weight and stay in Motion
A balanced diet and a lot of exercise and sport (30 – 60 min/day) are a healthy combination. The right weight furthers well-being and health.
Thermals, directional effectiveness, digestive power
There are various criteria for judging the effectiveness of herbs and foodstuffs.
The use of certain herbs and ingredients is based on observations of the effects on the body which these foodstuffs, herbs and spices show after

having eaten them. The medical science has developed following system: Every ingredient or herb has a directional effectiveness. Furthermore, there are herbs which have a special effect on certain organs.
The basic condition for a healthy metabolism is to obtain sufficient energy from food and that the digestive process doesn't use too much energy. An easily digestible meal makes content and sated, doesn't cause flatulence and fatigue after the meal. The perfect spices increase the healthiness of our meals. Very often, just small doses of herbs and spices will suffice. They are not used to make us sated, but to help our digestive organs to digest the food.

12.2 Recipes

The recipes list the ingredients to be used and the cooking instructions show how the dish is prepared. The list of ingredients shows the concerned quantities as well as the relevance for the therapy. If you find „omit", try to comply or find an alternative from the „list of recommended foodstuffs". Mostly it shall result just in a small change of taste when you simply avoid this ingredient.
Mild cooking methods: boiling, stewing, poaching, steaming
Strong cooking methods: barbecuing, roasting, frying, smoking
Balanced cooking methods: deep-frying, baking brick
Deep-freezing and warming in the microwave oven should be avoided (denaturalization).

12.3 Foodstuffs

Foodstuffs have an effect on body and soul like medicinal herbs, only a very much milder one. Dietary advice is mainly based on regional foodstuffs. The knowledge about the effects of each foodstuff and the knowledge, when which foodstuff shall be used, is based on the school medicine. Use ecologic-organic products, if possible. As everything should be cooked for a long time due to a better digestability and very rarely eaten raw, the food agrees with everyone.
The classification of the foodstuffs according to their effect on the body is the basis in order to achieve a harmonious status of health.
Dietary advisors do not recommend certain foodstuffs for everyone. The individual diet is tailor-made for the individual constitution.

Buy only fresh and ripe fruit and vegetables. You ought to leave unripe fruit and vegetables and such with brown spots and wilted leaves behind in the market. In this case take deep-frozen goods (never ready-to-serve dishes!). Fruit and vegetables are deep-frozen immediately after harvesting and often contain more vitamins and minerals than the goods from the vegetable shelf. Whereas conserved or tinned goods contain very much less biological substances. Also, salt, sugar and others are mostly added to the latter. Never leave the foodstuffs in the water after washing them to avoid that many vital substances get drowned. Clean salads, fruit and vegetables immediately before serving.

Please make sure of the hygienic processing of foodstuffs. Clean your salads, fruit and vegetables carefully. When cooking with meat, prepare all ingredients first and then process the meat products. Clean the worktop and tools very carefully. Wooden surfaces ought to be treated with a mild disinfectant regularly in order to reduce germination. Store fruit and vegetables separately, if possible. Harvested fruit and vegetables are still alive and emit e.g. ethylene gas, which makes other products ripen and age faster. Keep meat and fish in the closed packaging or store them in the fridge in closed containers.

12.4 Herbs

There are some basic rules for storing medicinal herbs. On principle, herbs must be protected from direct sunlight, humidity and heat.

Containers for the storage of herbs may be glasses, ceramic jars and even plastic containers. However, plastic is a rather unsuitable material and should only be a short-term solution. In case of glass containers, use a dark material.

Medicinal herbs cannot be kept for any long period. The shelf life of herbs is limited. However, it can be prolonged with suitable storage. The place should be dark, rather cool and absolutely dry. A wooden medicine cabinet, placed not directly next to a source of heat, would be ideal. Never buy large quantities of herbs so as not to have to throw them away. Label the container with the name of the herb and the date of harvesting or processing.

13 Other dietic-books

The following syndromes of dietetics, TCM or for a therapy supplement for cancer are available.

Dietetics

E001. Nutrition of the infant - baby food
E002. Nutrition during lactation
E003. Nutrition in old age
E004. Nutrition of children and adolescents
E005. Nutrition of athletes
E006. Light weight
E007. Pregnancy
E008. Full food

Protein and electrolyte - kidneys
E009. (hemodialysis) dialysis treatment
E010. Acute renal failure
E011. Chronic renal insufficiency
E012. Nephrotic syndrome
E013. Kidney stones (nephrolithiasis)

Gastrointestinal tract - pancreas
E014. Acute pancreatitis (inflammation of the pancreas)
E015. Chronic pancreatitis (inflammation of the pancreas)

Gastrointestinal tract - small intestine and large intestine
E016. Acute obstipation (constipation)
E017. Chronic obstipation (constipation)
E018. Colon irritabile
E019. Diverticulitis
E020. Acquired lactose intolerance (lactose malabsorption)
E021. Fructose malabsorption
E022. Glutensensitive enteropathy (celiac disease)
E023. Colectomy
E024. Short Bowel Syndrome

Gastrointestinal tract - liver, gallbladder, bile ducts
E025. Acute and chronic hepatitis (inflammation of the liver)
E026. Cholelithiasis (bile stones)
E027. fatty liver
E028. cirrhosis

Gastrointestinal tract - Stomach and duodenal intestine
E029. Acute gastritis
E030. Chronic gastritis
E031. Stomach bleeding
E032. Ulcus ventriculi and duodenal ulcer
E033. Condition after gastric surgery

Gastrointestinal tract - oral cavity and esophagus
E034. Stomatitis
E035. Esophageal carcinoma (esophageal cancer)
E036. Refluosophagitis (heartburn)

Special diseases
E037. Phenylketonuria (PKU)
E038. Rheumatic joint diseases

Metabolism
E039. Obesity (overweight)
E040. Diabetes mellitus
E041. Eating disorders (underweight)

Fat metabolism
E042. Hypercholesterolaemia (increased cholesterol level)
E043. Hepatic Encephalopathy

Heart and circulation
E044. Arteriosclerosis (arterial calcification)
E045. Heart insufficiency
E046. Hypertension
E047. Hyperuricaemia and gout

Changed nutrient requirements
E048. In case of fever
E049. For malignant diseases
E050. After burns
E051. Radiation and chemotherapy

CANCER
E100. Pancreatic cancer
E101. Bladder cancer
E102. Blood cancer (leukemia)
E103. Breast cancer
E104. Colorectal cancer
E105. Gastric cancer
E106. Kidney cancer
E107. Esophageal cancer

TCM
E200. Bladder - moisture heat in the bladder
E201. Bladder - moisture and cold in the bladder
E202. Bladder - emptiness and cold in the bladder
E203. Large intestine - external cold affects the large intestine
E204. Large intestine - moisture heat in the large intestine
E205. Large intestine - heat blocks the intestine II acute
E206. Large intestine - dryness of the colon
E207. Large intestine - Yang deficiency (cold)
E208. Heart - Blood insufficiency
E209. Heart - Blood stagnation
E210. Heart - Fire
E211. Heart - Hot mucus clogs the heart pores
E212. Heart - Cold mucus clogs the heart pores
E213. Heart - Qi deficiency
E214. Heart - Yang deficiency
E215. Heart - Yin deficiency
E216. Liver - Ascending Liver Yang
E217. Liver - Blood deficiency
E218. Liver - Blood stagnation
E219. Liver - Moisture heat in liver and gall bladder

E220. Liver - Fire
E221. Liver - Gall bladder Qi-Empty
E222. Liver - Cold in the liver meridian
E223. Liver - Qi stagnation
E224. Liver - Wind
E225. Liver - Wind with ascending liver Yang
E226. Liver - Wind with blood anemic
E227. Liver - Wind with extreme heat
E228. Lung - Qi deficiency
E229. Lung - Mucus-moisture in the lungs
E230. Lung - Mucus-heat in the lungs
E231. Lung - Mucus-cold in the lungs
E232. Lung - Dryness of the lungs
E233. Lung - Wind-heat attacks the lungs
E234. Lung - Wind-cold affects the lungs
E235. Lung - Yin deficiency
E236. Stomach - Bloodstagnation
E237. Stomach - Fire
E238. Stomach - Cold with liquid
E239. Stomach - Nutrition stagnation
E240. Stomach - Qi deficiency
E241. Stomach - Rebellious Qi
E242. Stomach - Yin Emptiness
E243. Spleen - Heat and moisture attack the spleen
E244. Spleen - Coldness and moisture affects the spleen
E245. Spleen - Qi deficiency
E246. Spleen - Qi deficiency + Declining spleen Qi
E247. Spleen - Qi deficiency + spleen does not control the blood
E248. Spleen - Yang deficiency
E249. Kidney - Heart and kidney no longer communicate
E250. Kidney - Jing deficiency
E251. Kidney - Kidneys cannot receive the Qi
E252. Kidney - Qi is not stable
E253. Kidney - Yang deficiency
E254. Kidney - Yin deficiency

For further information visit nutribook.info.

14 EBNS - Software for nutritional counseling

The main task of the database is to create personalized nutritional advice for each patient individually. The database was developed for Dietetics and Traditional Chinese Medicine.
The Database supports training and advices in the daily work routine.

The computer program provides lists of recipes, ingredients and herbs, which are given to the client. individually adjustable according to patient's request from whole food to vegetarians (lacto, ovo, ...). For every register there is an information sheet which can be given to the client. All texts can be individually designed.

The syndromes can be combined and result in an intersection of the recommended recipes and ingredients. The automated diagnosis for the TCM enables you to check your experience during the training as well as to confirm your diagnosis in the working day. You select several predefined symptoms and have the program automatically display the relevant syndromes.

How to work with the database:
Select the patient / client, select one or more of the syndromes you diagnosed and print the folder.

You can change all values, create new symptoms or syndromes, develop recipes, change or adapt ingredients and herbs to your findings. In simple client management, all relevant data about the person is stored. You get an overview of the past diagnoses and the development of the course of the disease.

As a consultant you save a lot of time when you print out the recipe, food and herbal lists for the recognized syndromes and give them to the clients. You can use this time for a personal conversation. With the database, dieticians and nutritionists can view the nutrients and trace elements for each recipe and develop recipes for syndromes even with suggested ingredients.

All recipe and grocery lists can also be ordered from me as a combination of several diseases. I wish all readers good luck, health and happiness in life.
More information can be found at www.ebns.at.
Volunteer: www.krebsinfo.at
Josef Miligui